AUSTRIA

PHOTOGRAPHS BY ELIZABETH KRAMER

THIS IS PART OF THE VISITING SERIES.

VIENNA

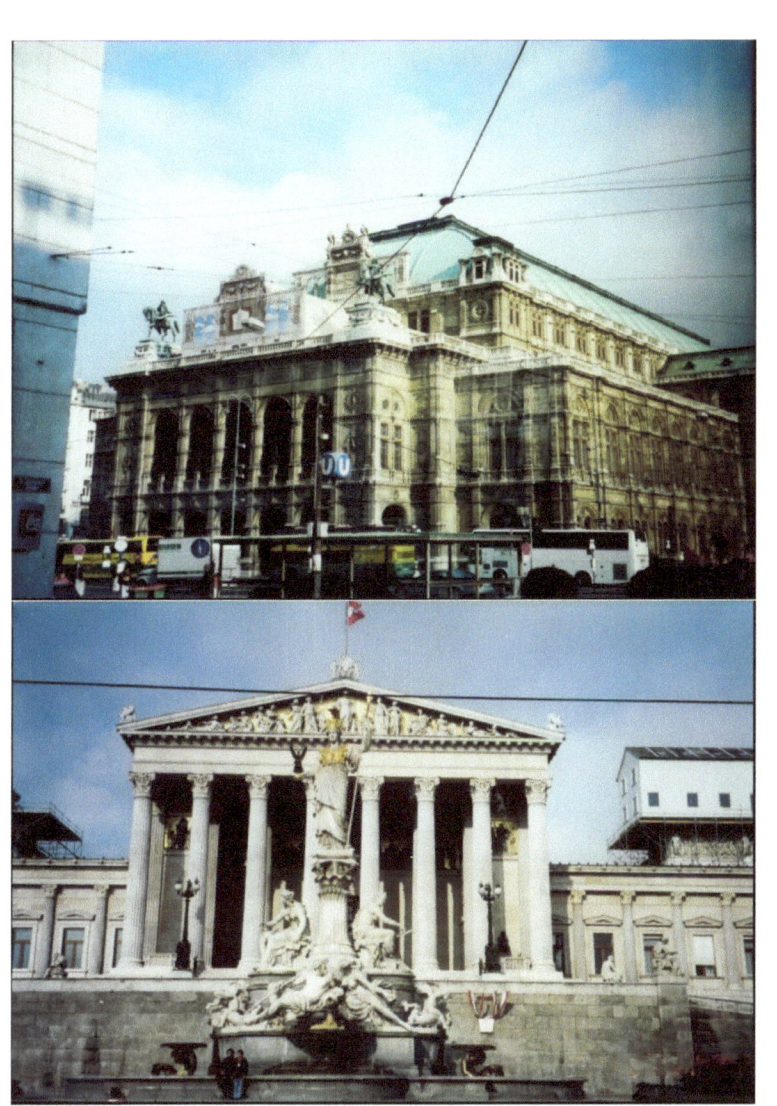

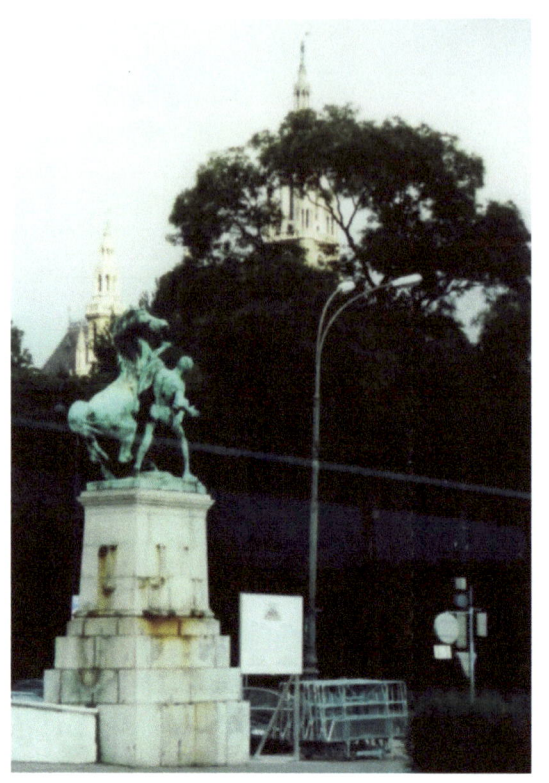

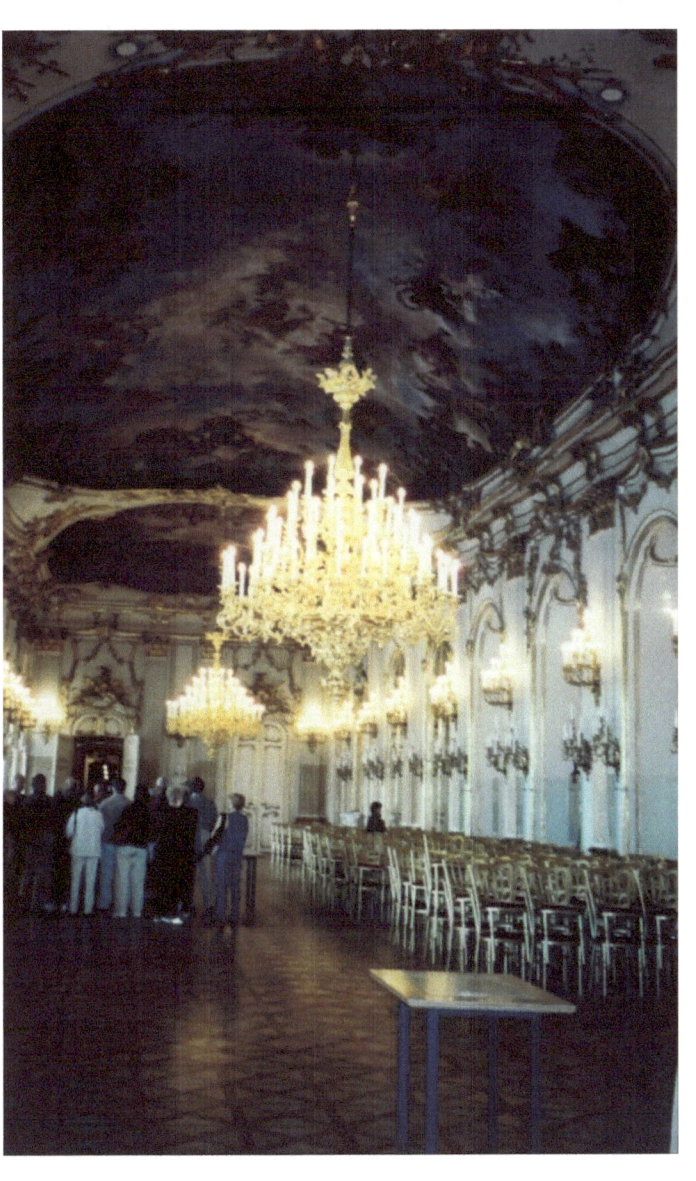

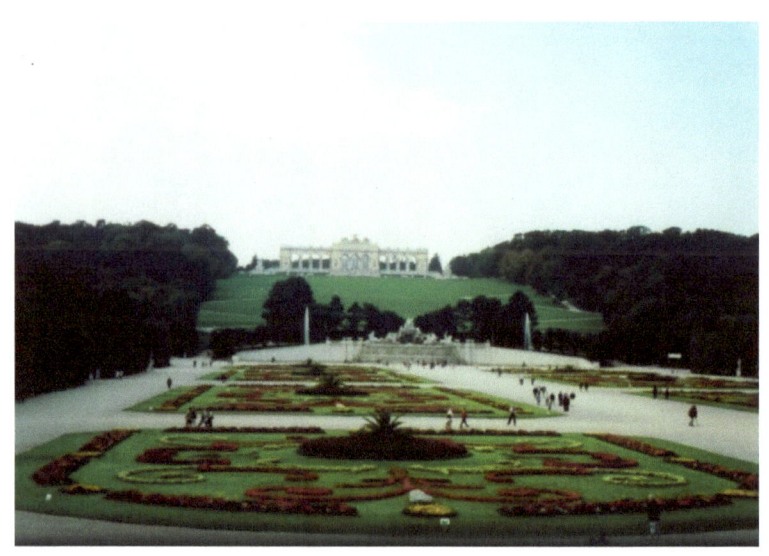

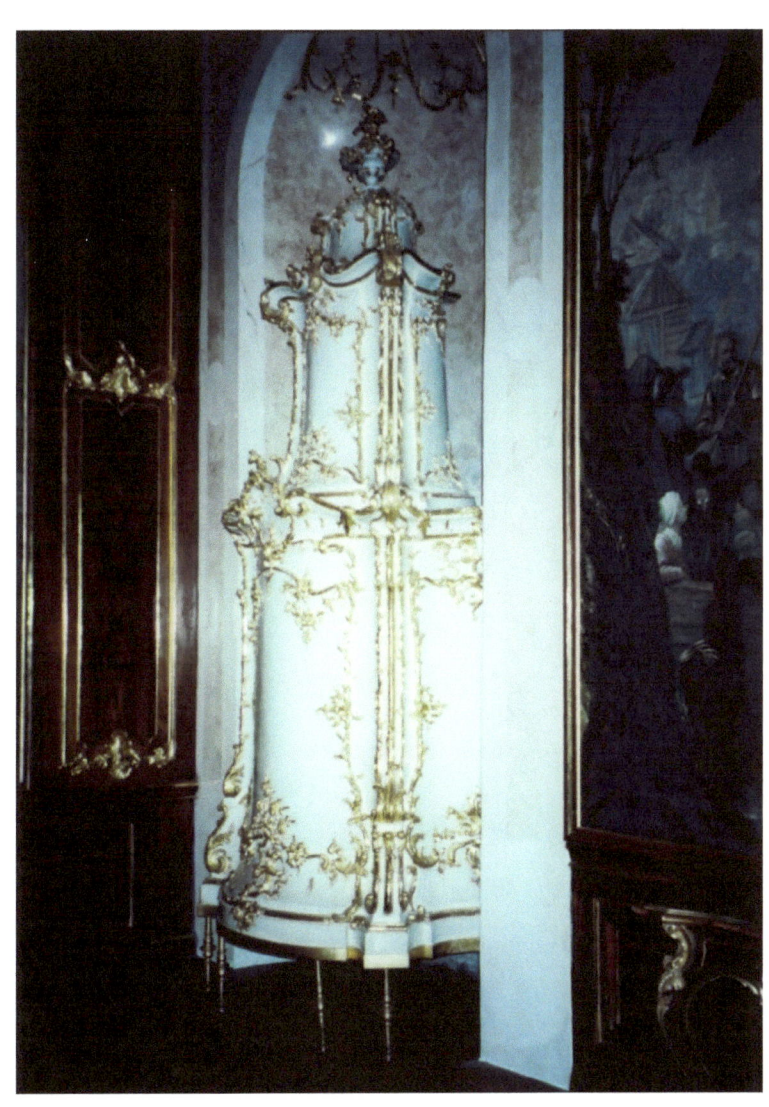

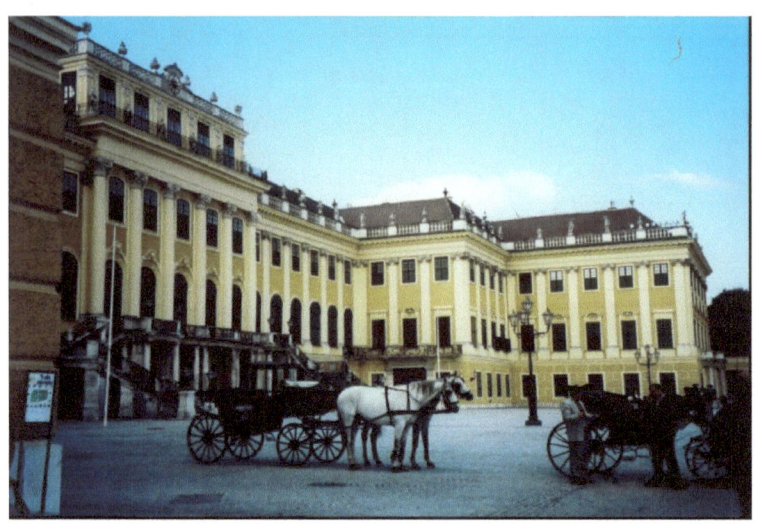

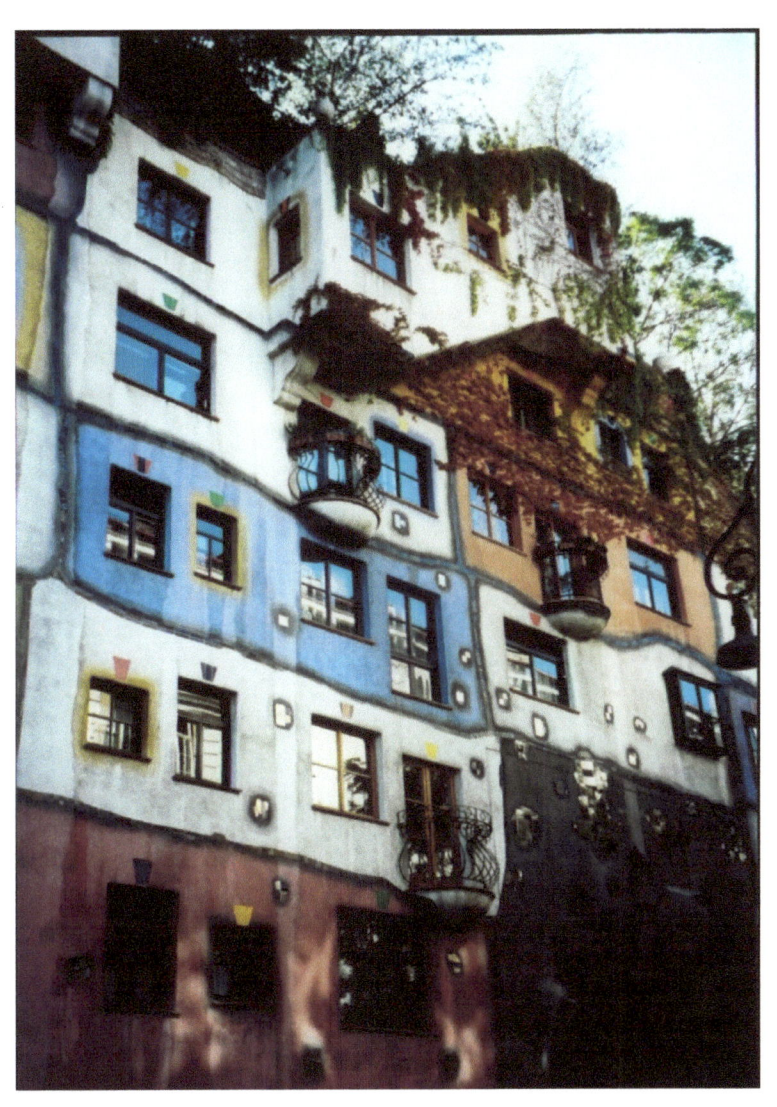

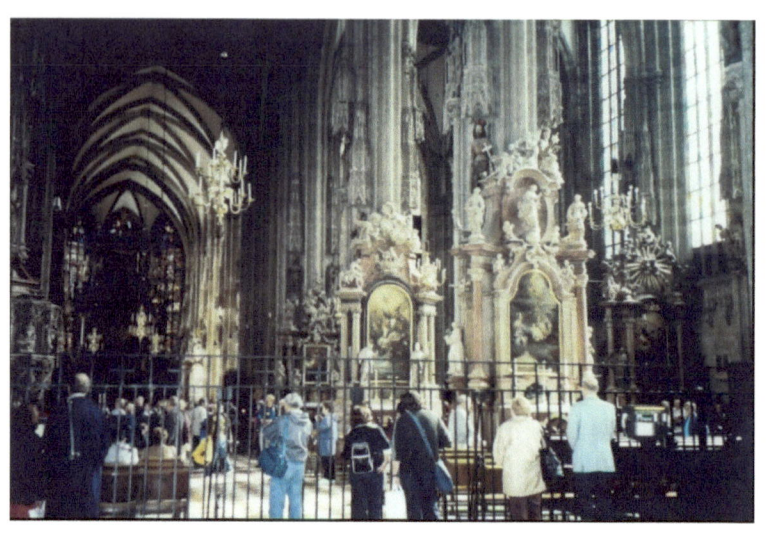

THE DANUBE

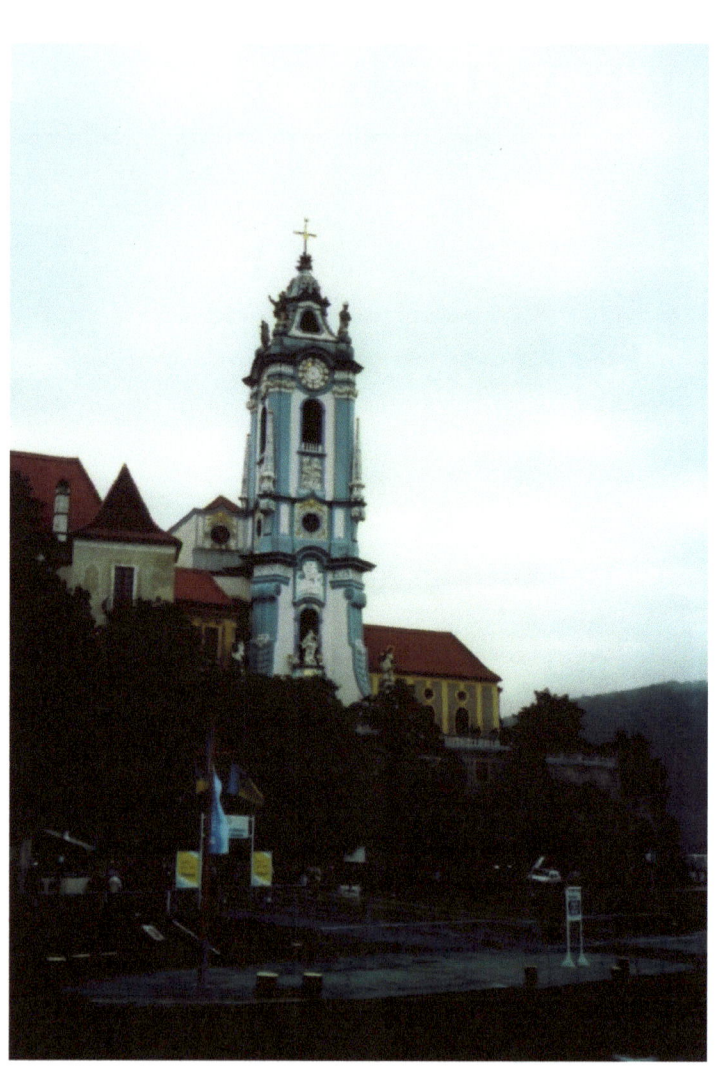

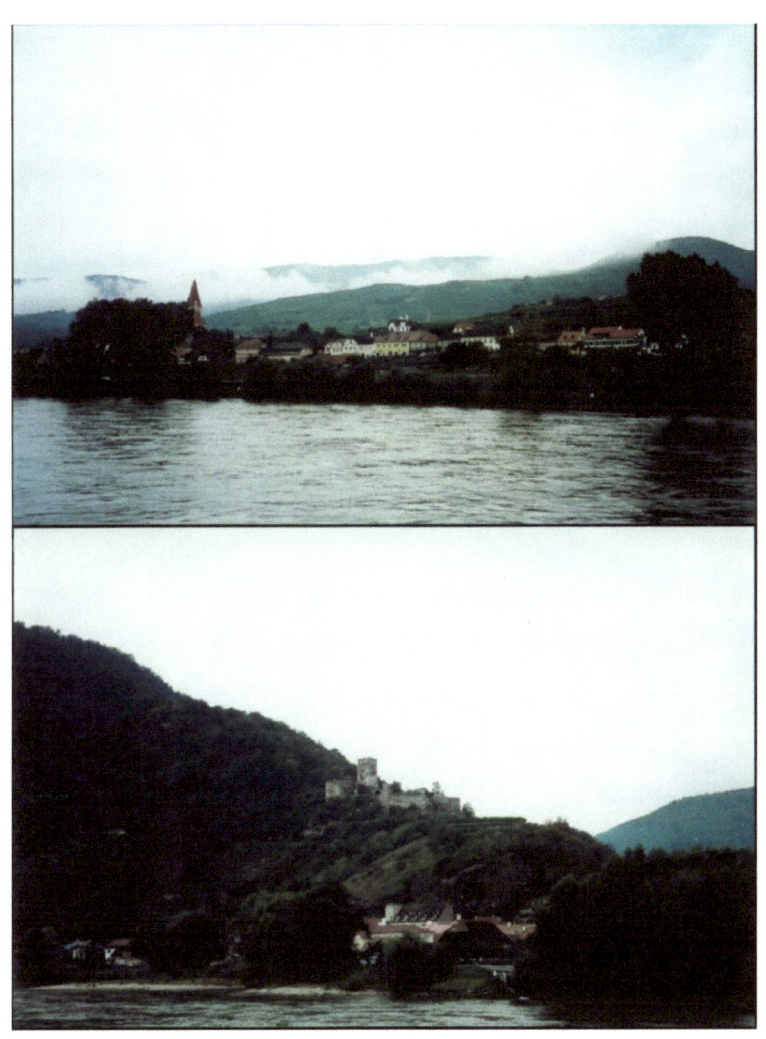

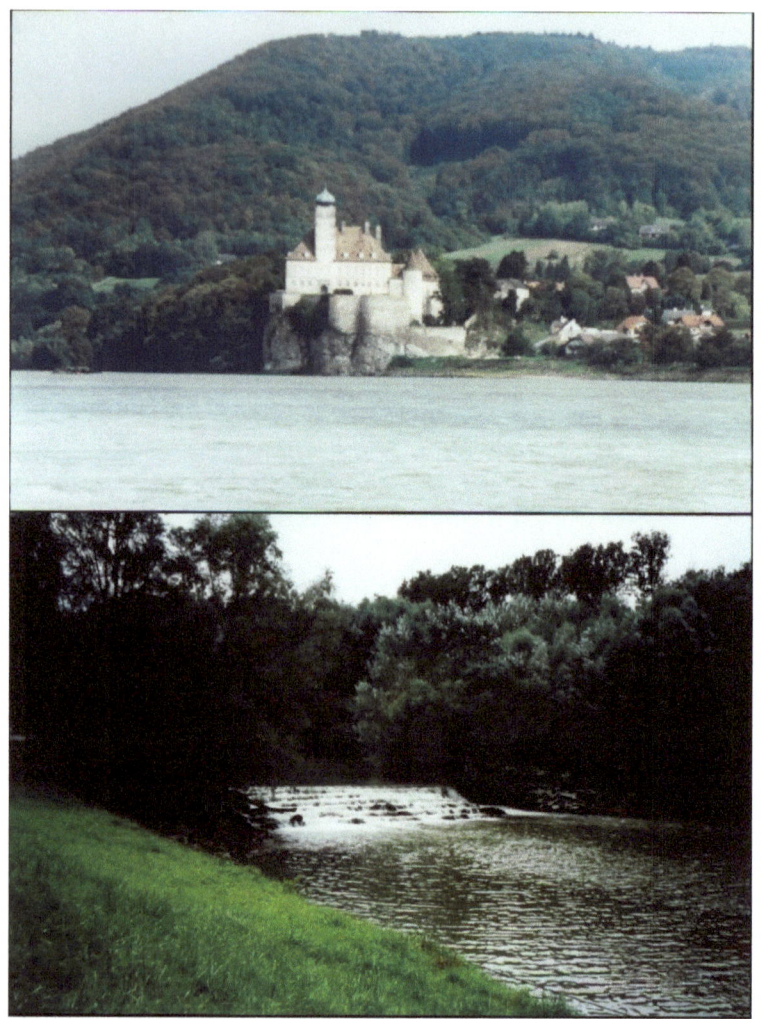

MELK ABBEY

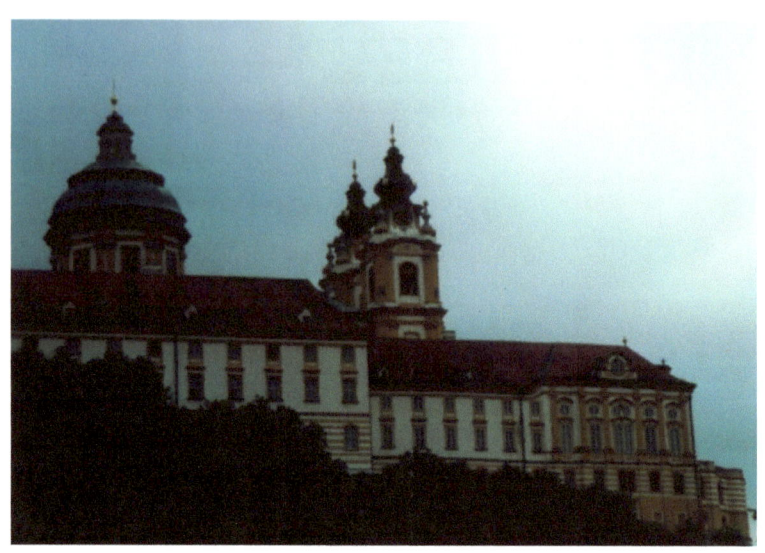

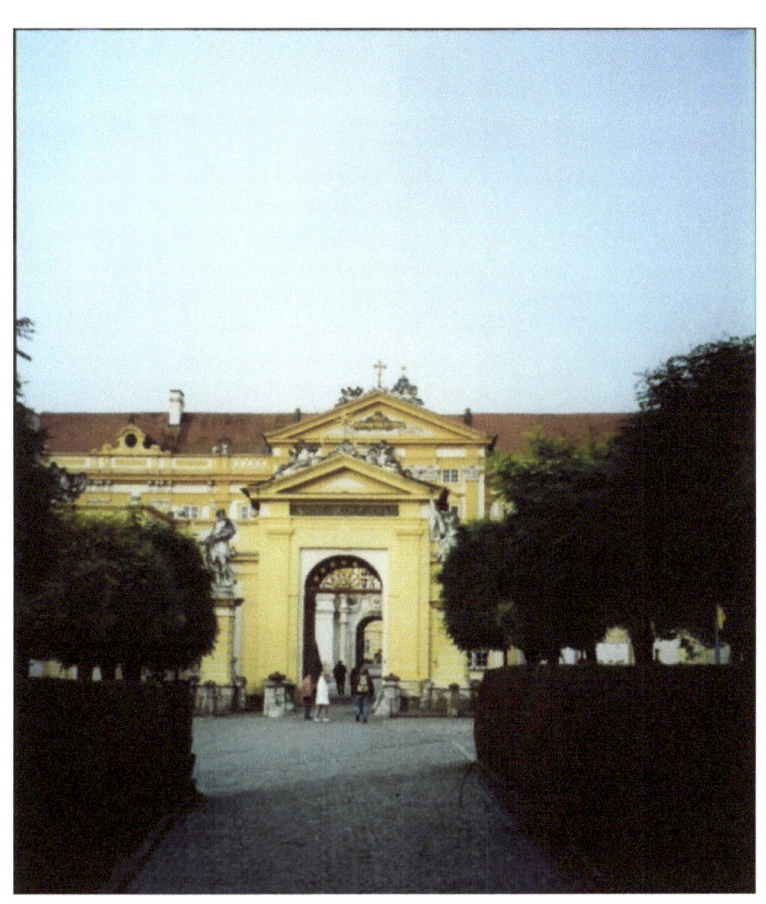

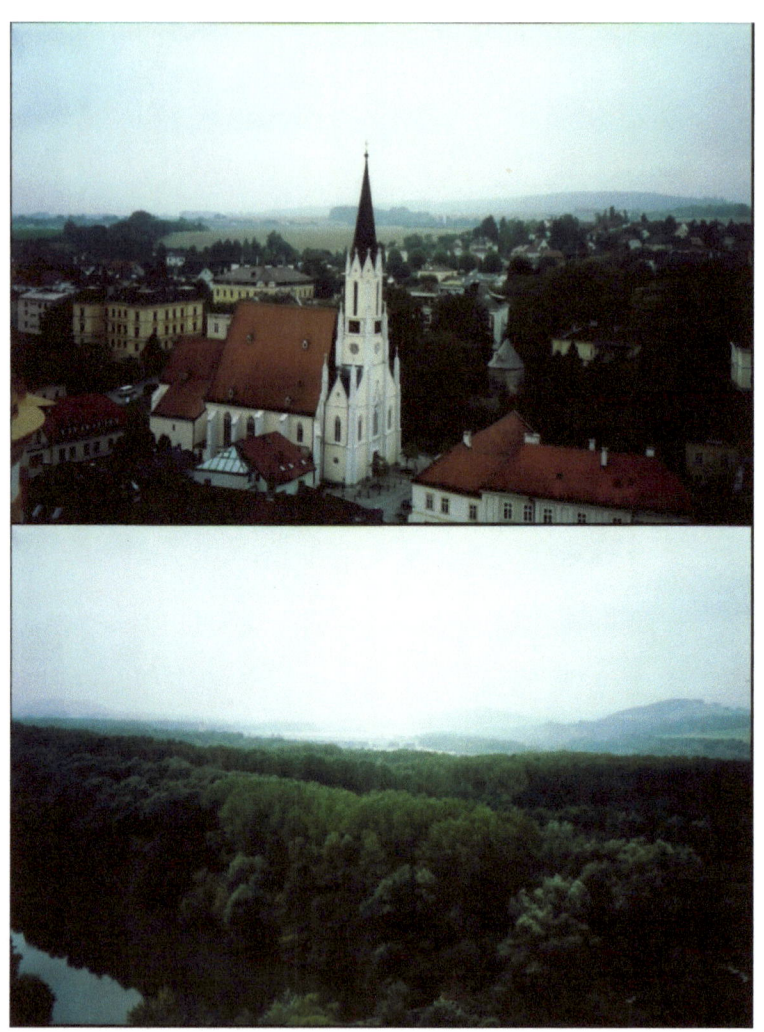

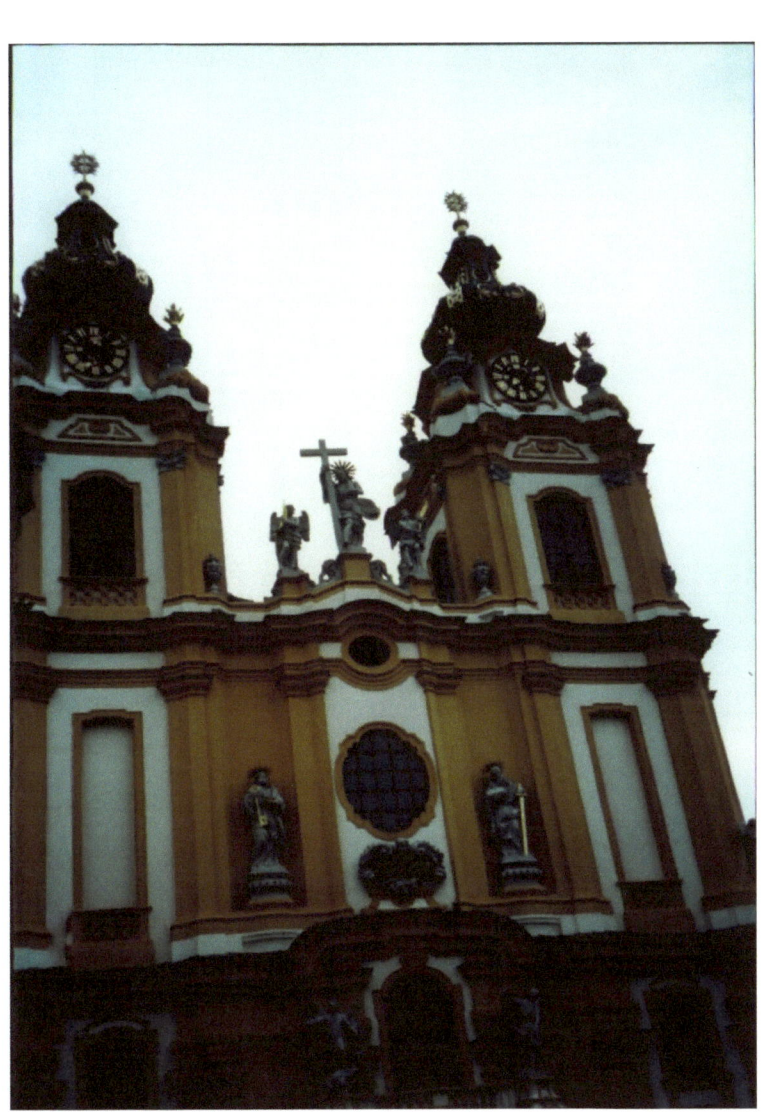

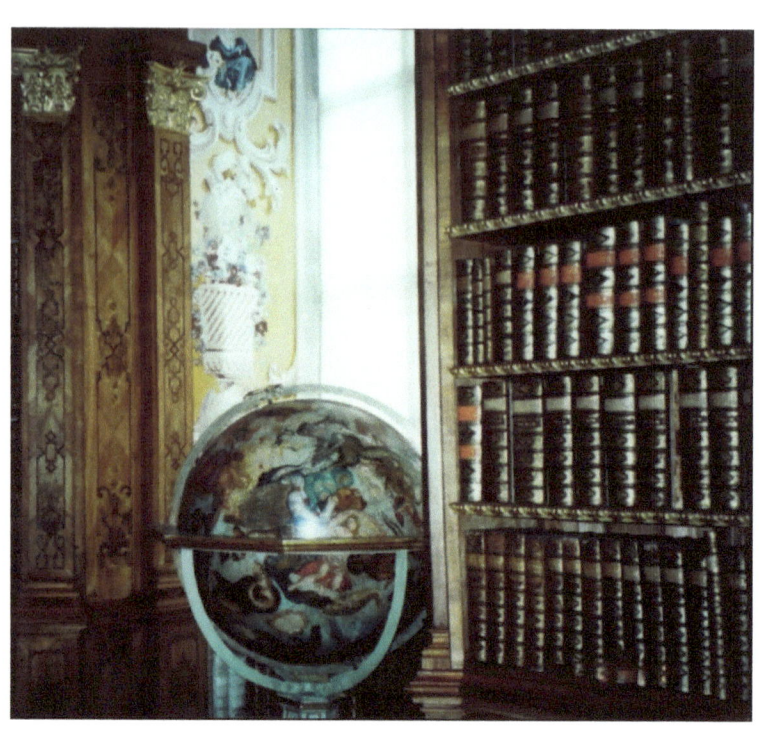

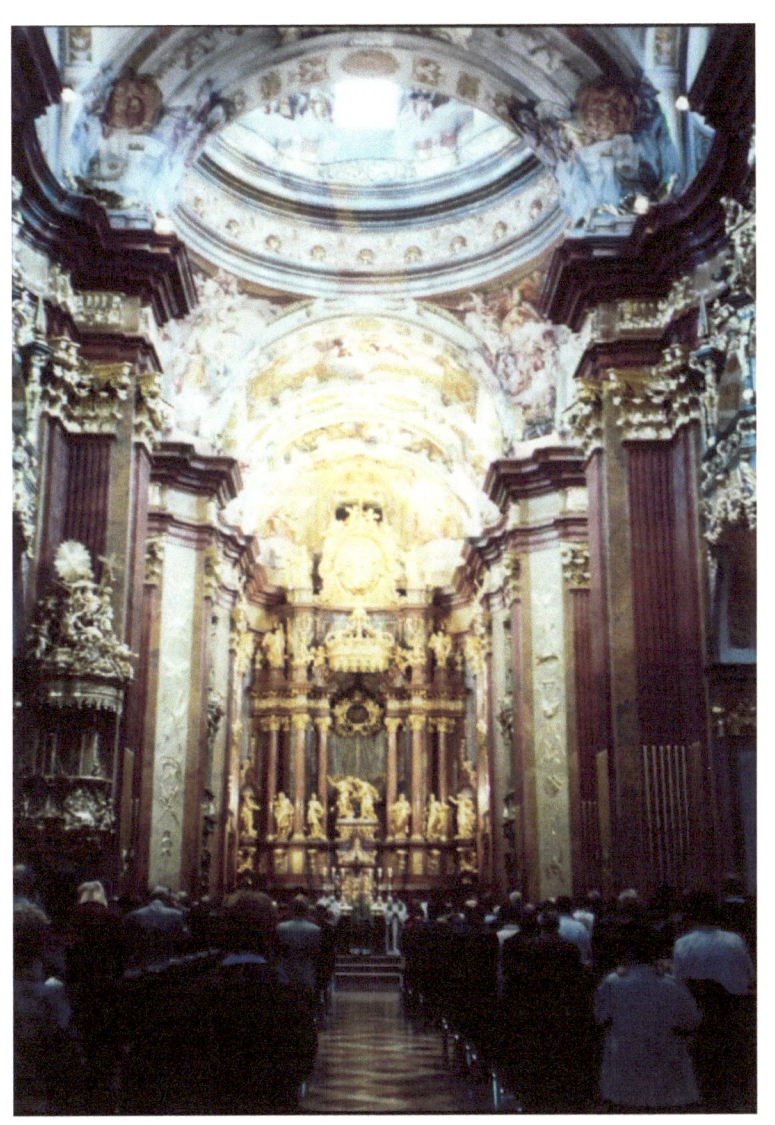

SALZBURG

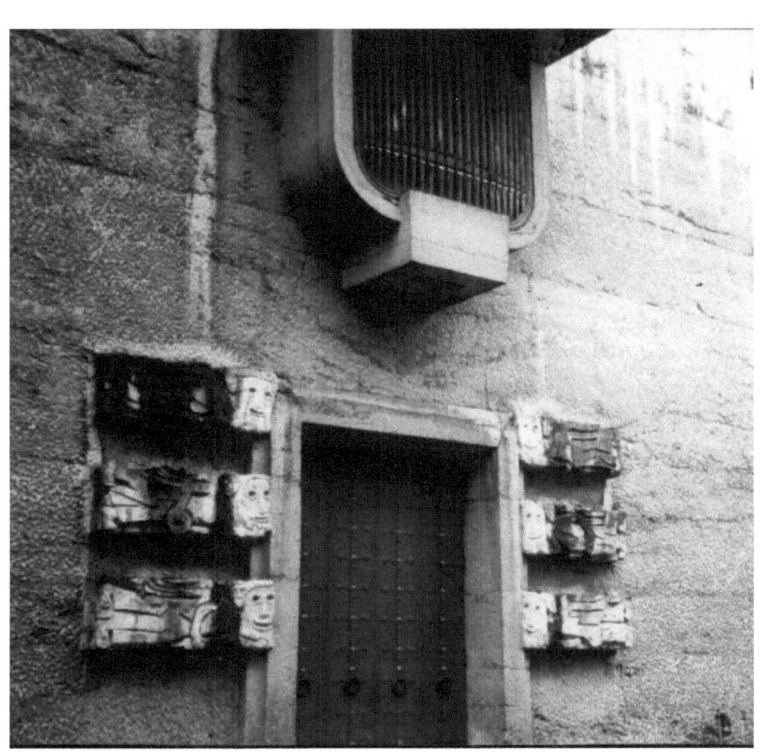

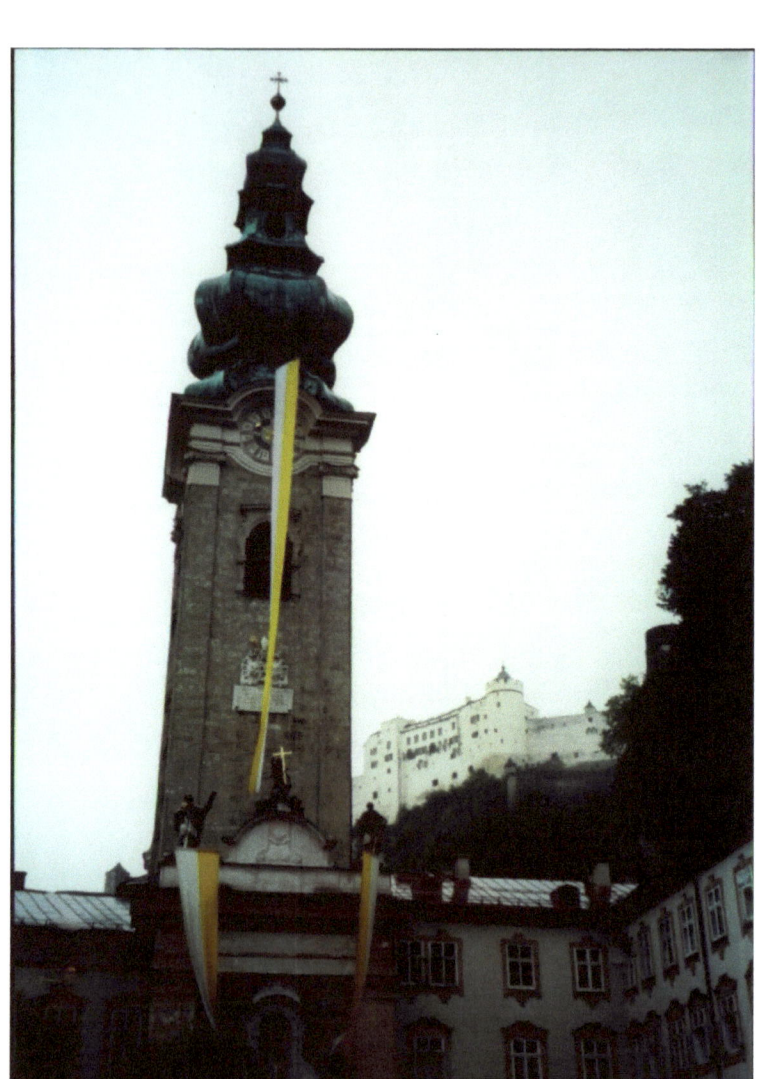

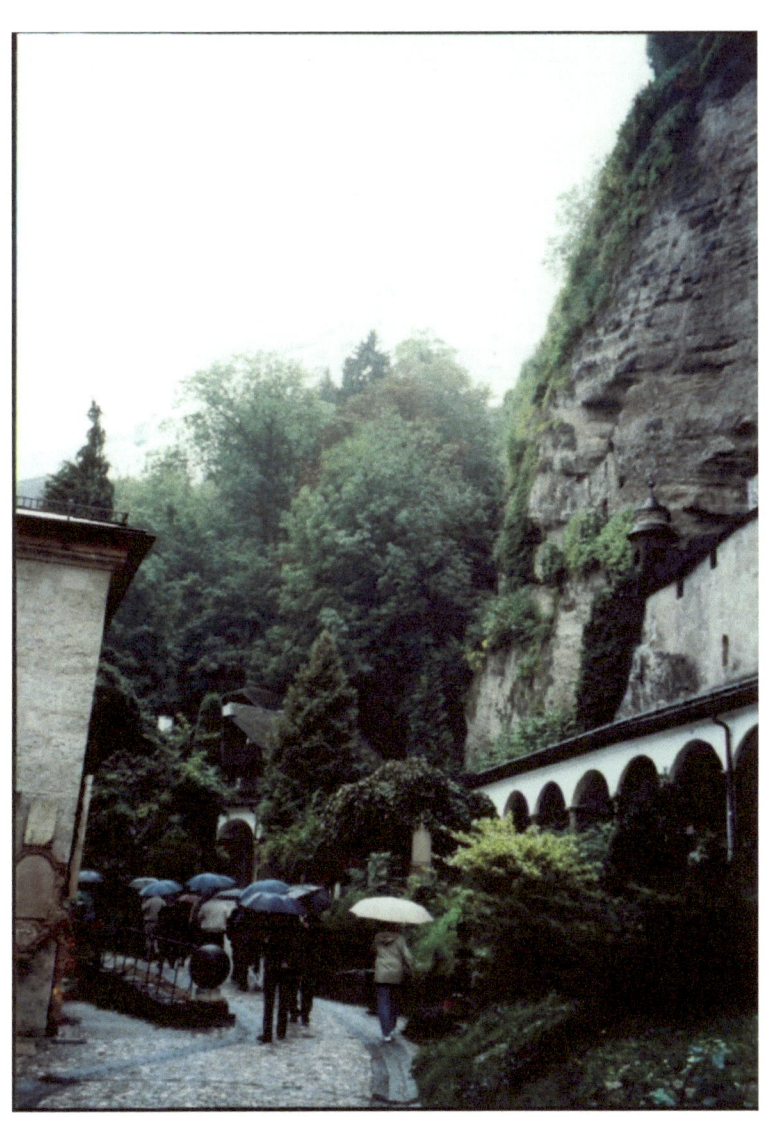

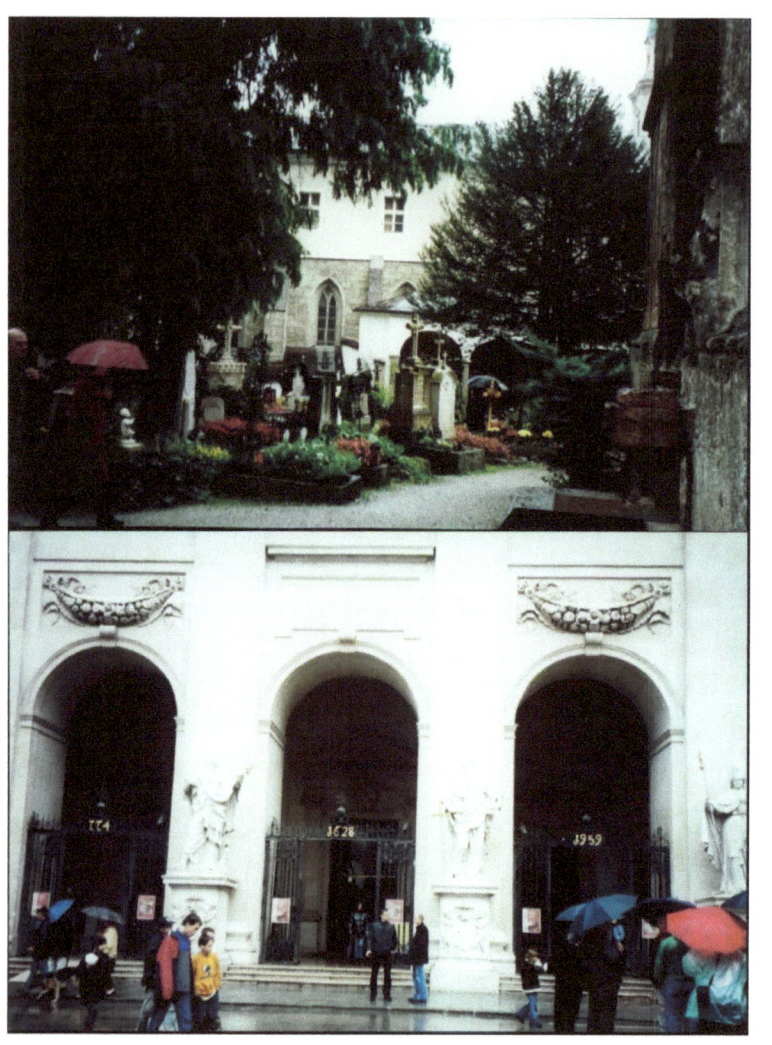

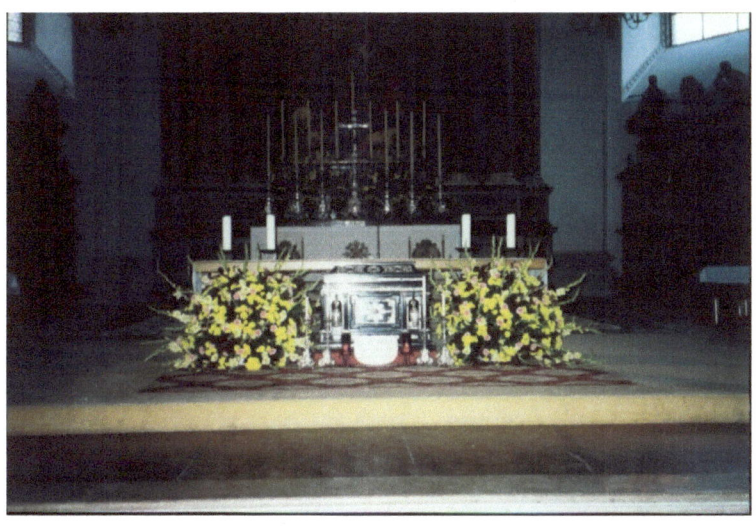

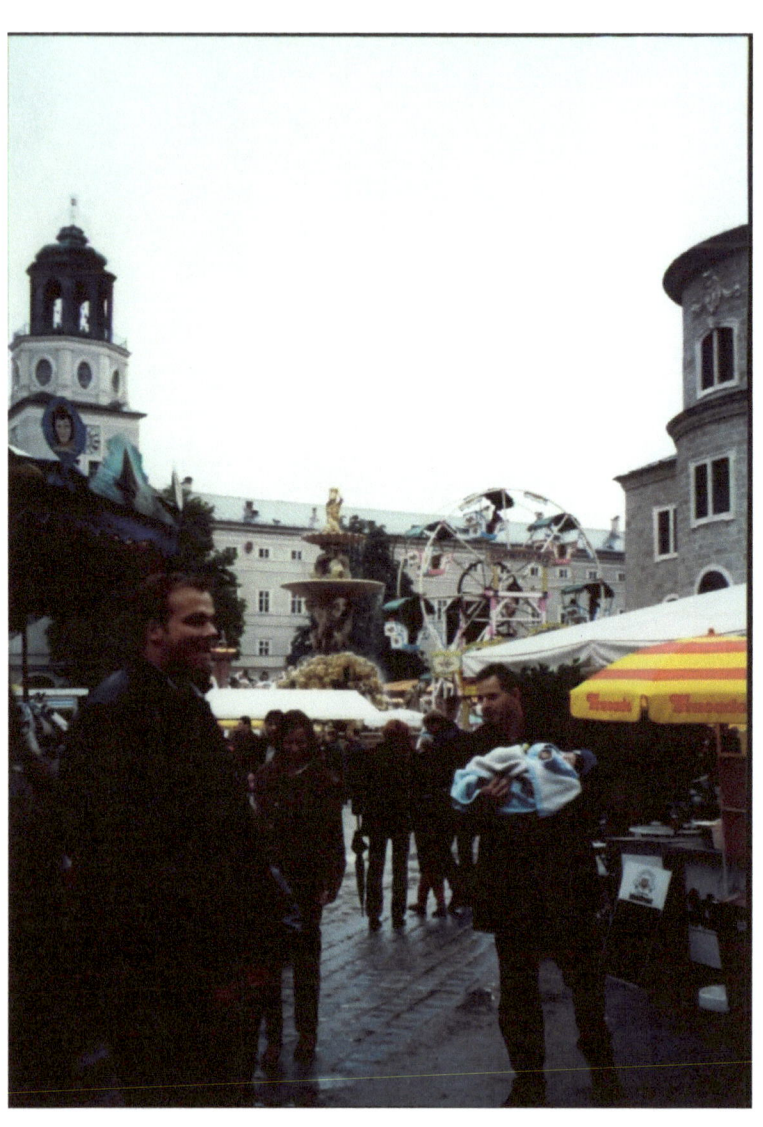

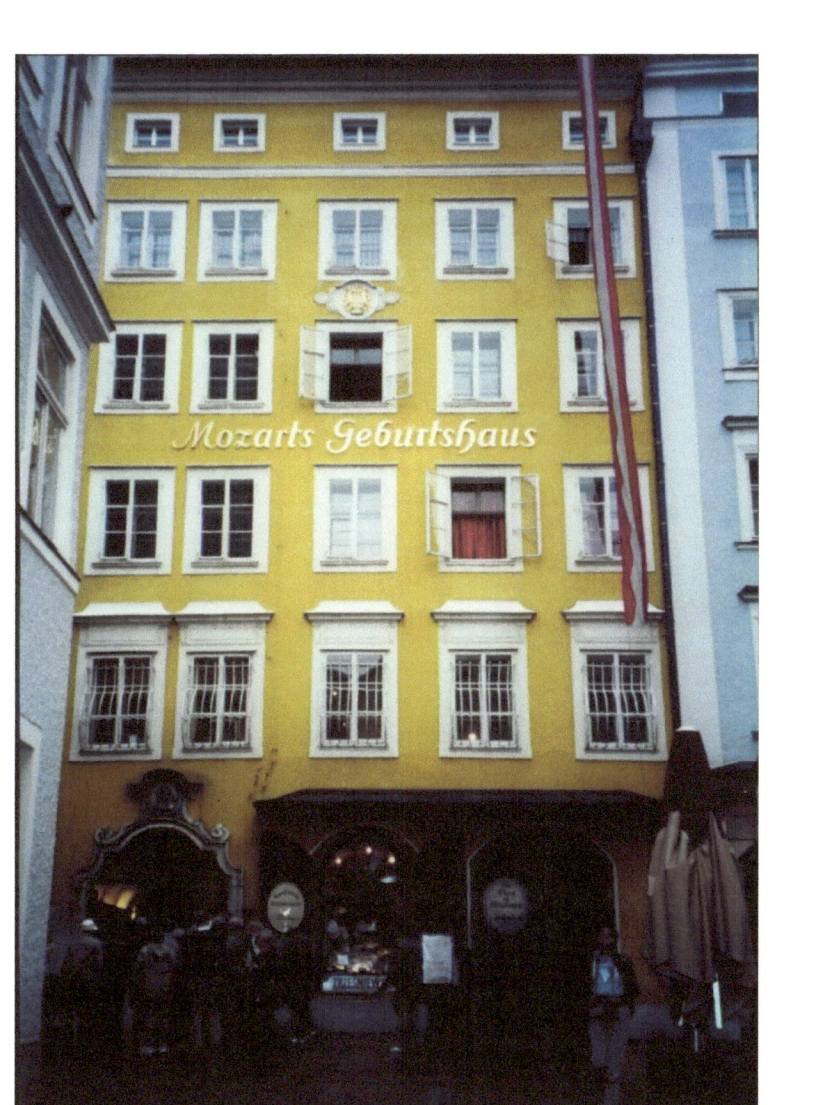

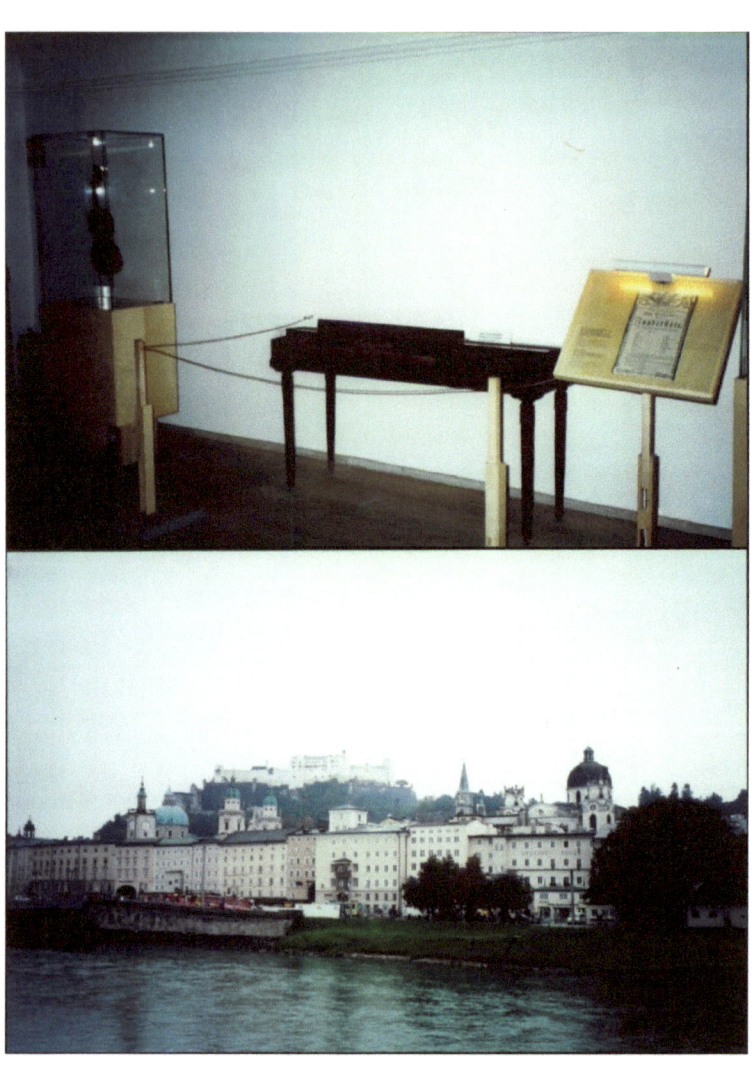

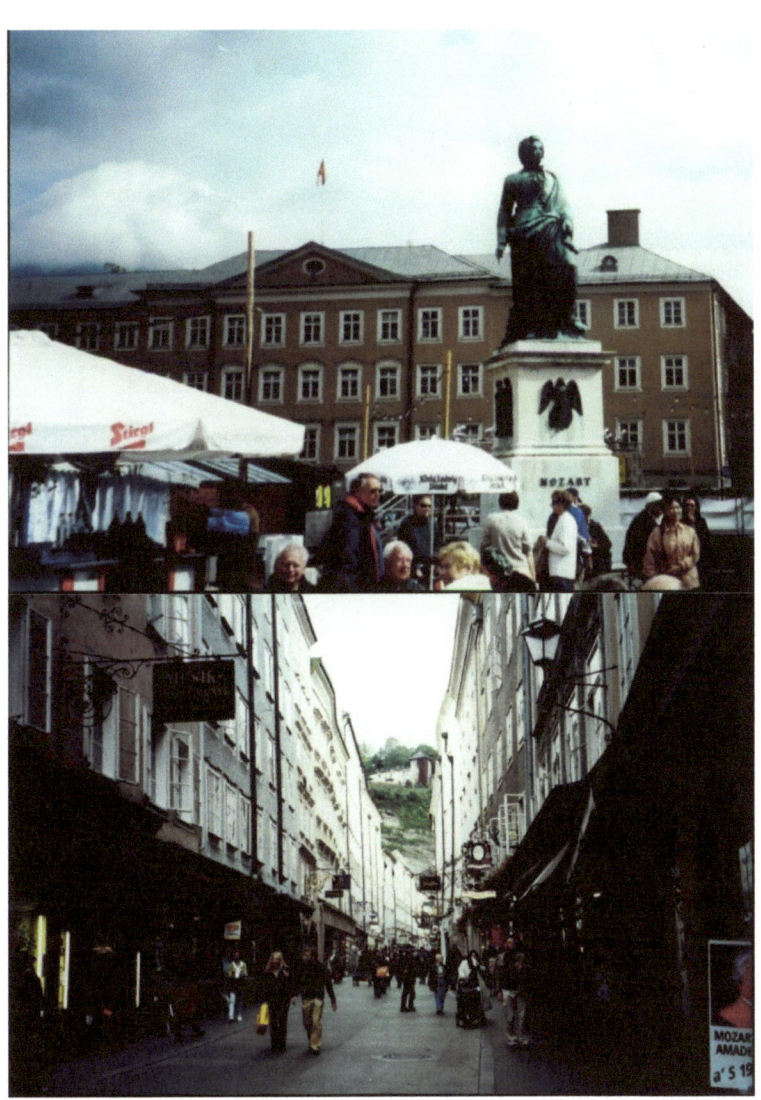

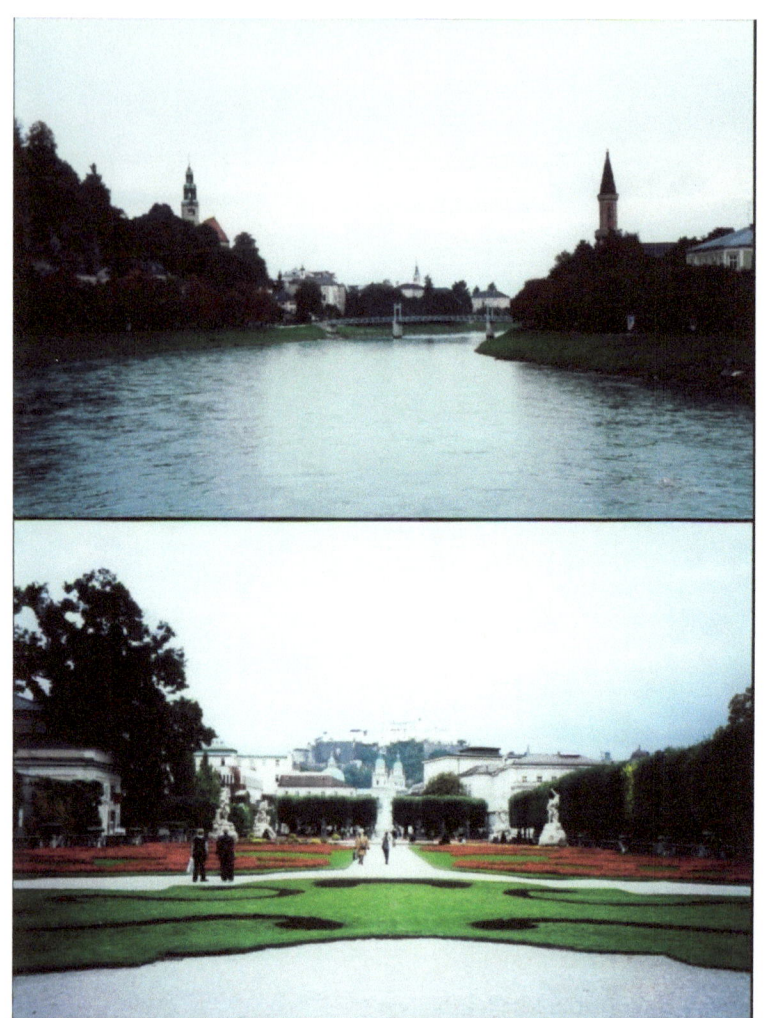

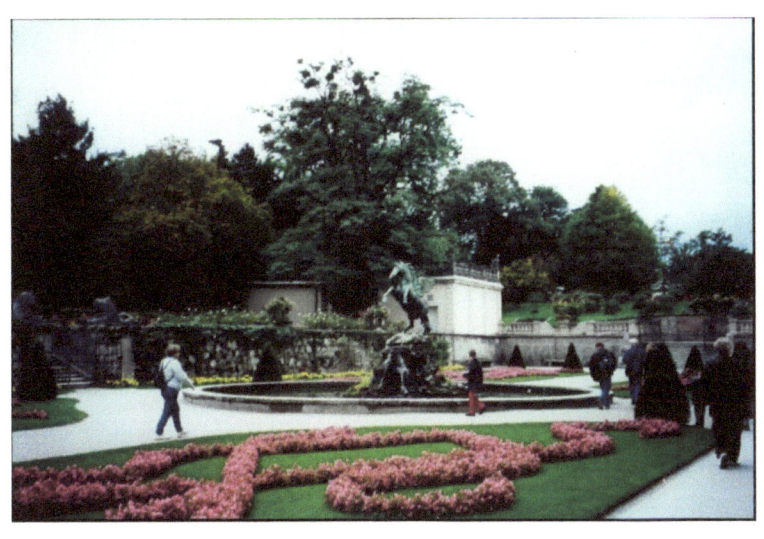

INNSBRUCK

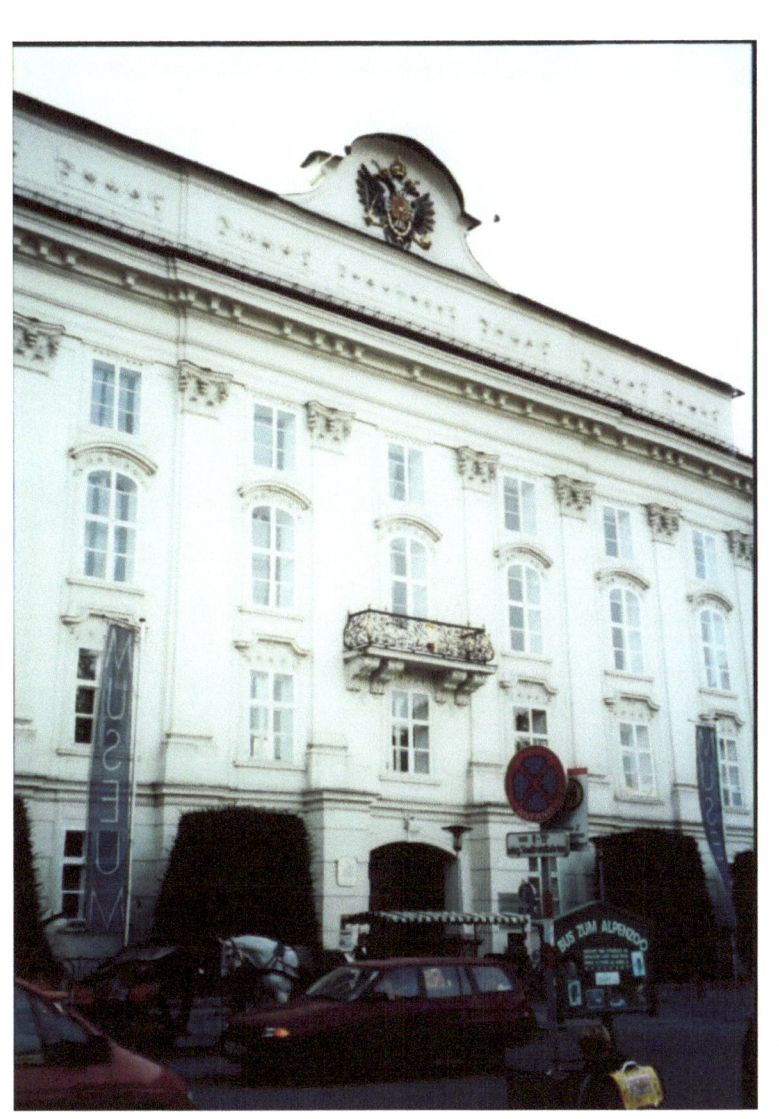

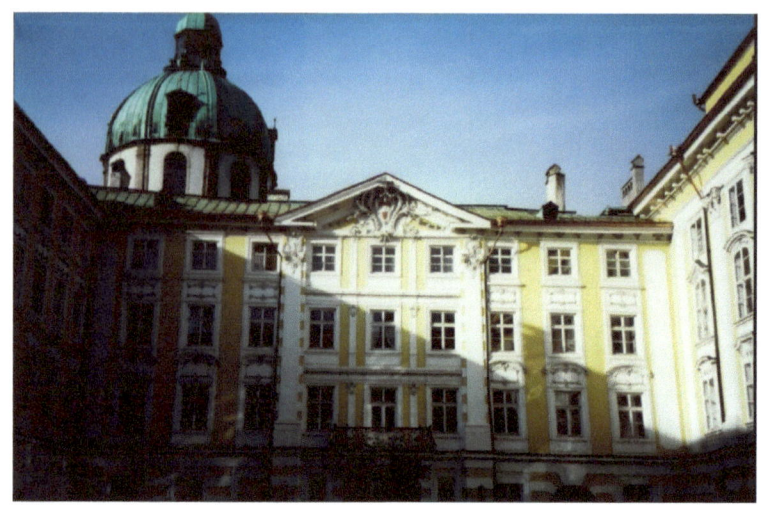

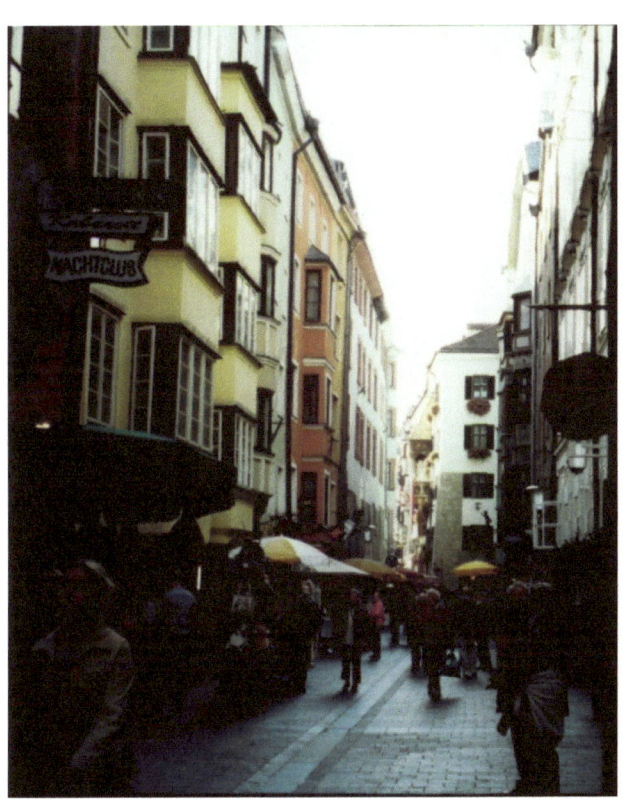

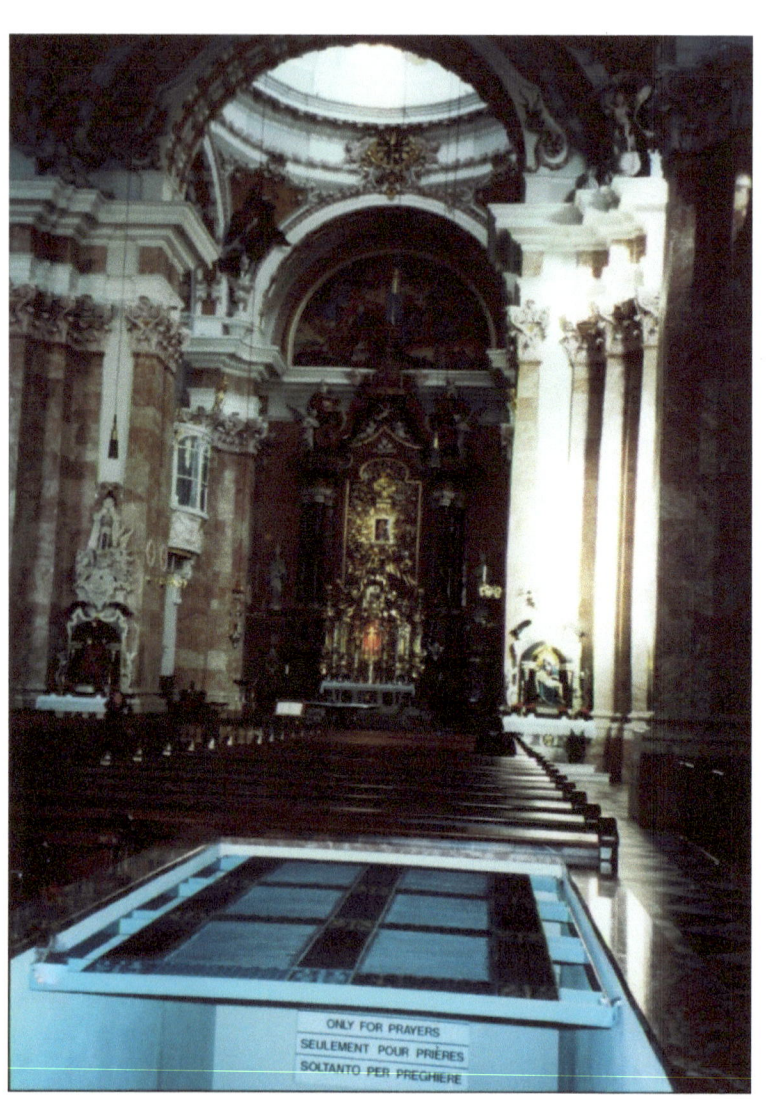

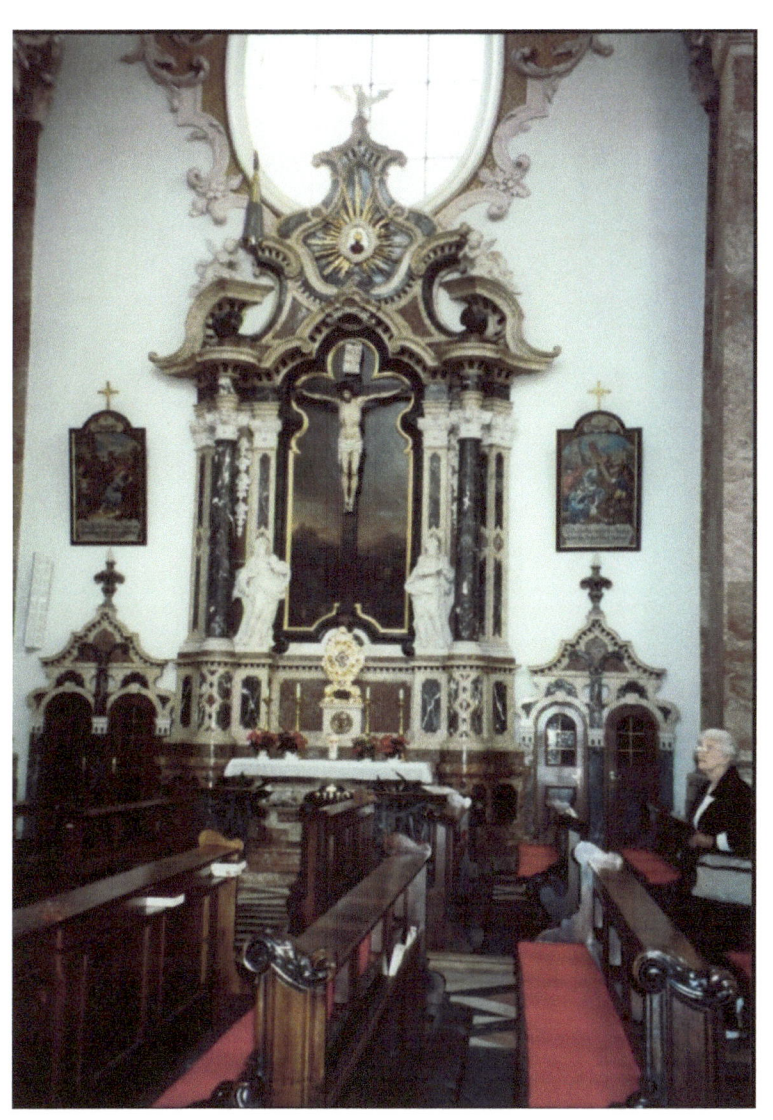

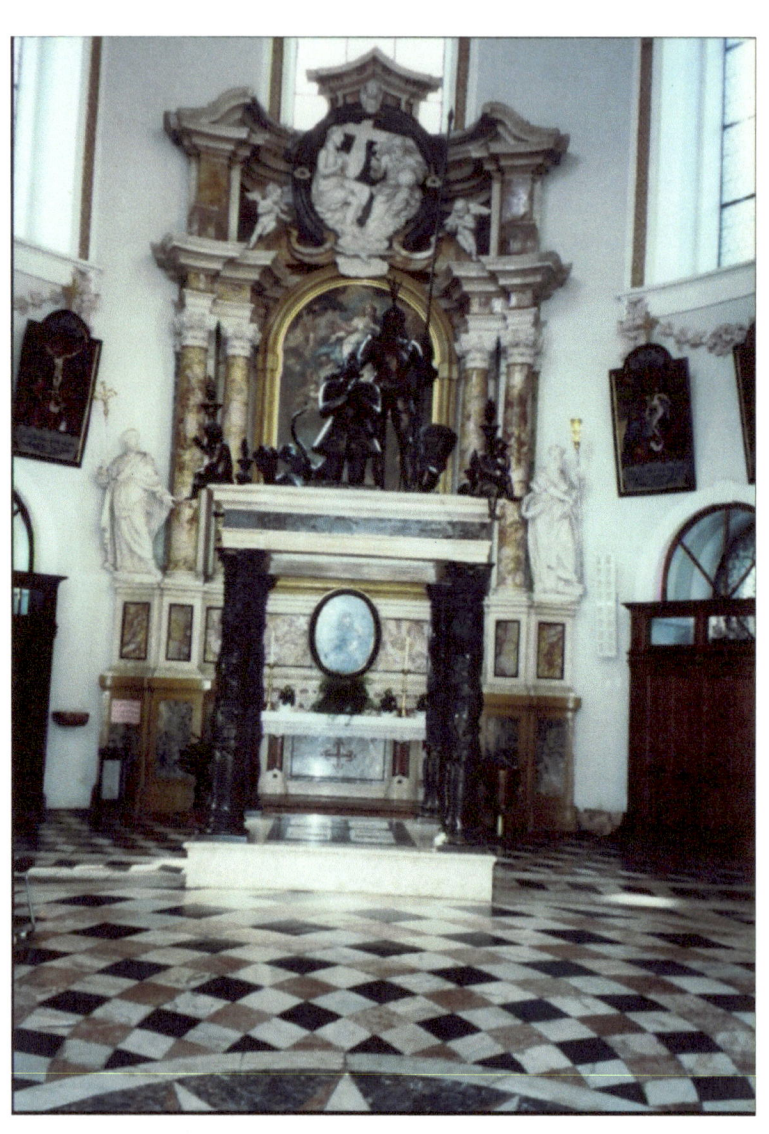

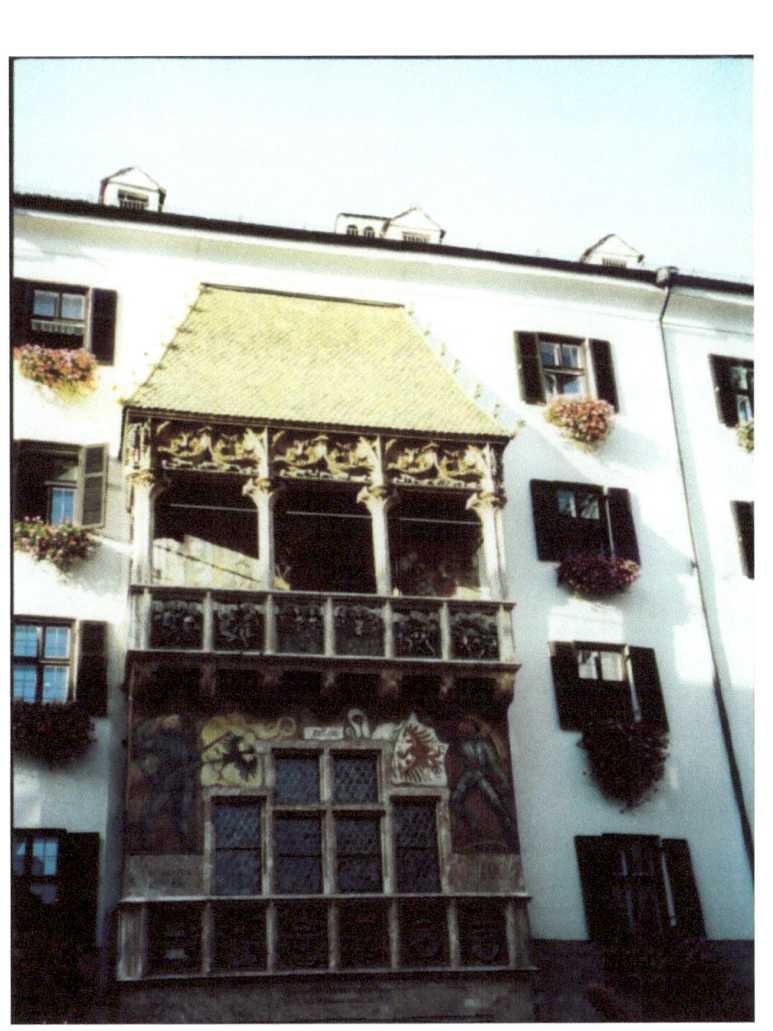

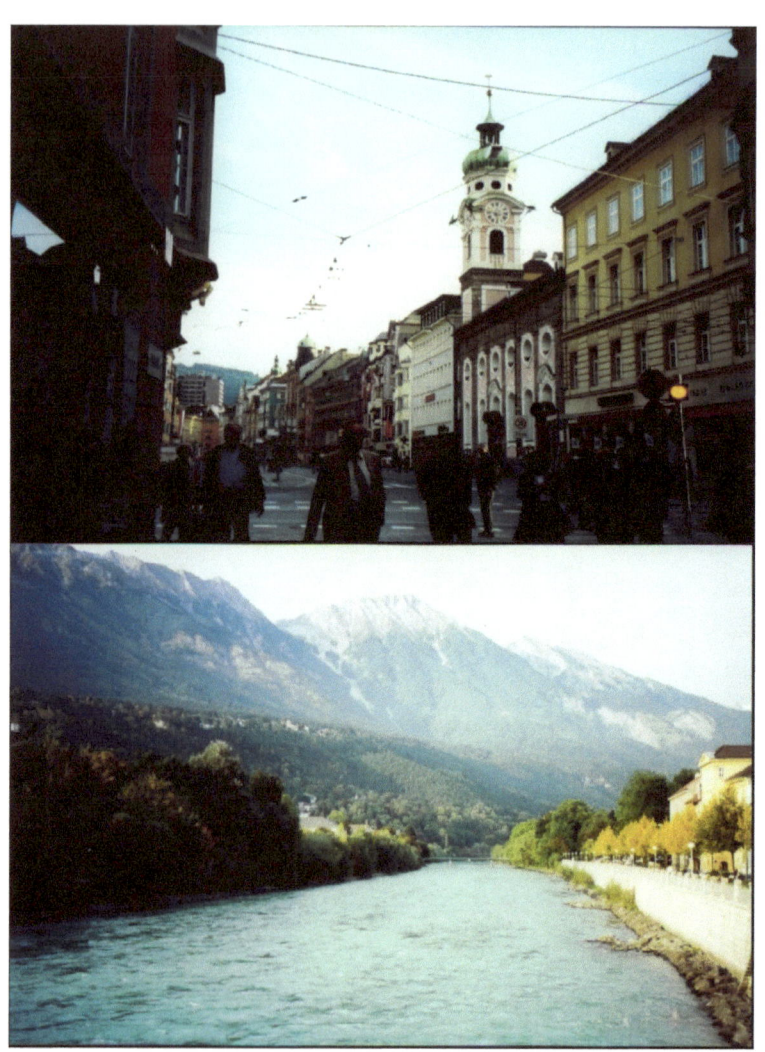

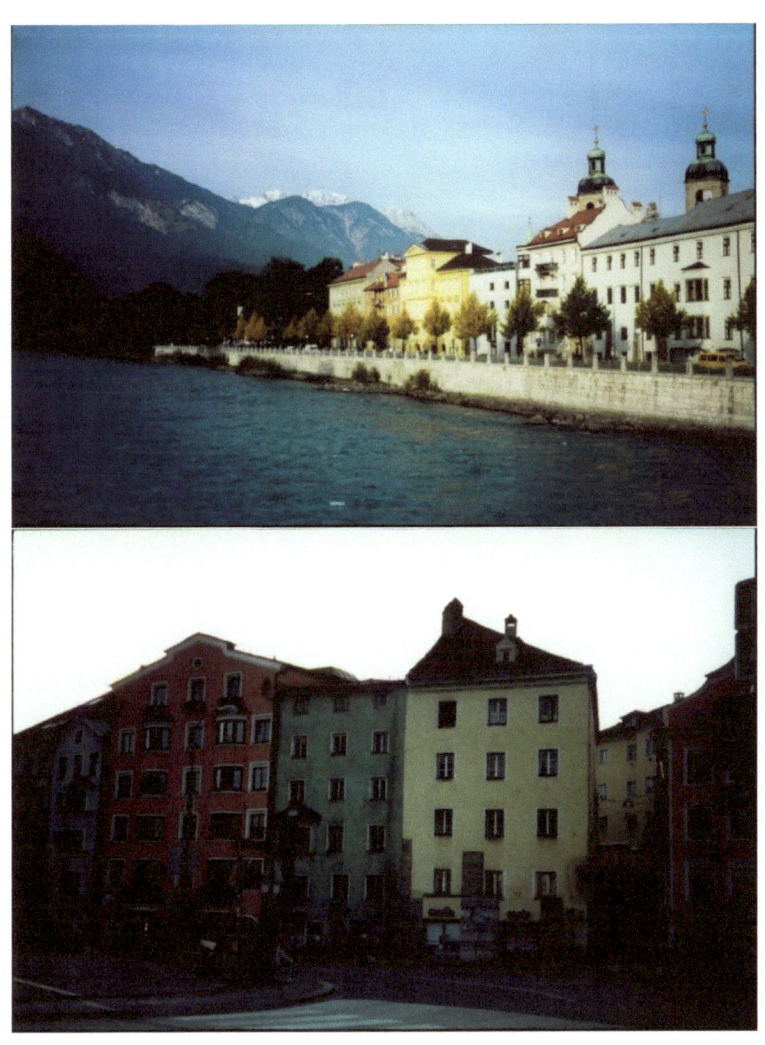

www.ingramcontent.com/pod-product-compliance
Lightning Source LLC
Chambersburg PA
CBHW040928180526
45159CB00002BA/655